Disclaimer

The publisher of this book is by no way associated with the National Institute of Standards and Technology (NIST). The NIST did not publish this book. It was published by 50 page publications under the public domain license.

50 Page Publications.

Book Title: An Analytical Approach to Cost-Effective, Risk-Based Budgeting for Federal Information System Security

Book Author: Barbara C. Lippiatt; Sieglinde K. Fuller

Book Abstract: The purpose of this report is to identify and illustrate an approach to simplify and strengthen capital planning for information system security in compliance with federal policy and guidance. The report provides the theoretical underpinnings of a methodology that will enable budgeting officials, system owners, and managers to select cost-effective strategies for optimizing the level of information system security to be achieved, given the level of vulnerability faced by the organization. The method of evaluation used is the Analytic Hierarchy Process (AHP), a multi-attribute decision approach. It integrates quantitative and qualitative information in a hierarchical structure in such a way that decision-makers can logically and consistently evaluate all the alternatives in a complex decision problem. An illustrative case study applies the AHP to the selection of a cost-effective security investment, given the likelihood and magnitude of threats to the information system. Expert judgments of risks, overall agency goals, and existing system weaknesses are merged with investment costs to illustrate the AHP process for calculating a measure of merit for evaluating investment alternatives.

Citation: NIST Interagency/Internal Report (NISTIR) - 7385

Keyword: Building Economics, Economic Impact Analysis

NISTIR 7385

An Analytical Approach to Cost-Effective, Risk-Based Budgeting for Federal Information System Security

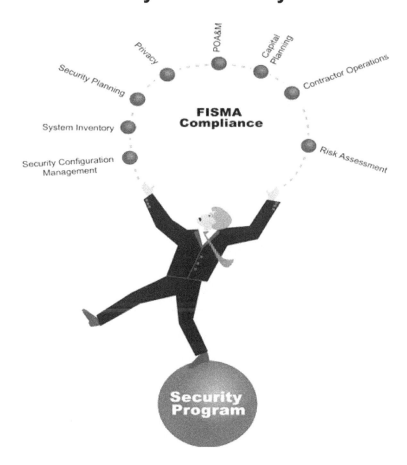

Barbara C. Lippiatt
Sieglinde K. Fuller

January 2007

National Institute of Standards and Technology
Technology Administration, U.S. Department of Commerce

National Institute of Standards and Technology
Technology Administration, U.S. Department of Commerce

An Analytical Approach to Cost-Effective, Risk-Based Budgeting for Federal Information System Security

Barbara C. Lippiatt
Sieglinde K. Fuller
Office of Applied Economics
Building and Fire Research Laboratory
National Institute of Standards and Technology
Gaithersburg, MD 20899-8603

January 2007

U.S. Department of Commerce
Carlos M. Gutierrez, *Secretary*

Technology Administration
Michelle O'Neill, *Acting Under Secretary for Technology*

National Institute of Standards and Technology
Dr. William A. Jeffrey, *Director*

Abstract

The purpose of this report is to identify and illustrate an approach to simplify and strengthen capital planning for information system security in compliance with federal policy and guidance. The report provides the theoretical underpinnings of a methodology that will enable budgeting officials, system owners, and managers to select cost-effective strategies for optimizing the level of information system security to be achieved, given the level of vulnerability faced by the organization. The method of evaluation used is the Analytic Hierarchy Process (AHP), a multi-attribute decision approach. It integrates quantitative and qualitative information in a hierarchical structure in such a way that decision-makers can logically and consistently evaluate all the alternatives in a complex decision problem. An illustrative case study applies the AHP to the selection of a cost-effective security investment, given the likelihood and magnitude of threats to the information system. Expert judgments of risks, overall agency goals, and existing system weaknesses are merged with investment costs to illustrate the AHP process for calculating a measure of merit for evaluating investment alternatives.

Key Words: analytic hierarchy process, computer systems, cost-effective investments, economic analysis, information system security, IT investment budgets, multi-attribute decision tool.

Disclaimer

Acknowledgments

The authors wish to thank Elizabeth Chew, Marianne Swanson and Richard Kissel at the Computer Security Division (CSD) of the NIST Information Technology Laboratory for supporting this work. We are also grateful for the advice and information we received from Joan Hash (formerly of CSD), and Alicia Clay, CSD, during the earlier stages of this project. Stakeholders from various agencies also gave us valuable and much appreciated information in meetings and interviews throughout the year. Special appreciation is extended to Darren Smith, formerly of the NIST Enterprise Systems Division in Boulder, for providing technical advice during the preparation of the report. We also appreciate the help of Jeanne Springmann, Sean Sell and Joe Kau of the Applications System Division and Stan Morehouse of the Building and Fire Research IT Support Team in designing the case study. Dr. Harold Marshall, Dr. Robert Chapman, and Dr. David Butry, of the Office of Applied Economics (OAE), made many helpful suggestions. We also thank Ms. Julie Wean and Ms. Tessa Beavers of OAE for their help in producing the document, and Kevin Stine of the Food and Drug Administration for the cover graphic.

Contents

List of Tables

List of Figures

1 Introduction

1.1 Background

Protecting information systems from unauthorized access, use, disclosure, disruption, modification, and destruction can be extraordinarily expensive and impossible to ensure with 100 % confidence. Because the likelihood of a breach in an information system and the size of resulting costs are so uncertain, it is difficult for decision-makers responsible for security to make the case for investments in protection against such threats. It is even more difficult to optimize such security investments. While too little security poses obvious risks, too much security is also problematic. Excessive layers of protection against security breaches, for example, can slow system performance, lowering the productivity of agency staff and in turn impeding an agency from fulfilling its mission. Stakeholders want an optimal level of security that is a business enabler, not a business inhibitor. In other words, they want practical guidance on the best ways to protect their information systems from attack in a cost-efficient manner over the life cycle of the information system.

1.2 Purpose

The purpose of this report is to lay the foundation for simultaneously simplifying and strengthening capital planning for information system security by identifying and illustrating an approach enabling established, repeatable, automated processes that comply with federal policy and guidance. The intended audience includes members of Information Technology (IT) Investment Review Boards (IRBs)—consisting of capital budgeting officials and senior IT managers responsible for developing and justifying enterprise IT investment portfolios—as well as information system owners responsible for proposing security investments for IRB consideration. The approach helps decision-makers select cost-efficient strategies and security controls to achieve a level of information system security commensurate with the degree of risk and magnitude of harm.

Although the focus is on federal information system security, the approach described in this report is readily adaptable to private sector information system security. The same principles apply in the evaluation of any information system security investment seeking the proper balance of risk and cost.

1.3 Organization

The remainder of this report is organized into five chapters. Chapter 2 builds a common understanding by describing the context in which investments for information systems are currently made. Chapter 3 describes an approach well suited to support these investment decisions, followed by its suggested application to the security investment process in Chapter 4. In Chapter 5, the approach developed in Chapter 4 is illustrated in a case study. Chapter 6 summarizes and concludes the report by laying out possible next steps for implementation, automation, and dissemination of the approach.

2 The Capital Planning Environment for Federal Information System Security

For most federal agencies, there are four levels at which key investment decisions regarding information system security are made:

(1)   Information system owner/manager level
(2)   Enterprise level (e.g., offices, bureaus, and institutes belonging to Cabinet-level, or Executive, agencies),
(3)   Executive agency level, and
(4)   OMB level (for "Major" information system budget requests of $1 million or more)

This report presents a model for improving the decision-making process at the first three levels. Once a proposed, Major Investment is approved for submission to the fourth level, Office of Management and Budget (OMB), a number of additional financial analyses and justifications are required, such as return-on-investment (ROI) calculations and "alternatives analyses" documenting that the proposed investment is the most cost-effective one. Thus, it is important that the decisionmaking leading up to the OMB budget request be transparent and defensible. Yet at the same time it is not advisable to implement a model requiring all the rigor of an OMB-type analysis at the first three levels: it would be overly burdensome to require development of ROI measures for all alternatives under consideration at any stage of the process, many of which are never forwarded for OMB consideration because they are too small or are rejected at the enterprise or executive agency level. Thus, while the model presented in this report addresses the "investment" side of the ROI calculations, it does *not* address monetization of the "return", or benefit, side. Monetizing the benefits of information security investments is the subject of future research as discussed in Section 6.2.3.

To develop a common understanding of the environment in which investments for federal information system security are currently made, the rest of this chapter focuses on the requirements, realities, and need for improvements to decision-making at the system, enterprise, and executive agency levels.

2.1 System Level Requirements

In keeping with OMB reporting requirements, agencies are to maintain records for each of their information systems. These records contain data that can support investment decision-making. Among these data is the level of potential impact on organizations or individuals, should certain events occur that jeopardize the information and information systems needed by the organization to accomplish its mission. The impact levels, rated Low, Moderate or High, as defined in the Federal Information Processing Standard (FIPS) 199[1] describe the extent of the adverse impact if

---

[1] Federal Information Processing Standard 199, *Standards for Security Categorization of Federal Information and Information Systems*, February 2004.

the three overall information security goals of system confidentiality, integrity, and availability were breached. The information system is rated with respect to each security goal, and then the overall system impact is determined by taking the highest impact level among the three. This is known as the "high-water mark" approach.

Information system owners are responsible for the periodic assessment of the security controls implemented on their systems and for proposing to senior management investments to address any security weaknesses that are found. Those weaknesses are documented on the Plan of Action and Milestones (POA&M) that is reported to OMB.

2.2 Enterprise and Executive Agency Level Requirements

At the enterprise level, system owners are to identify, and propose for funding, any information security investments applicable at the enterprise architecture level, without reference to specific systems. These investment proposals are combined with the system-based proposals from throughout the enterprise, as well as with non-security-related information system investment requests, and prioritized for funding requests. Most enterprises, depending on size, have either formal or informal IRBs, consisting of senior information system managers, and perhaps capital planning staff, that make these prioritizations. While limited by increasingly tight budgets, the IRB is also faced with having to consider the degree to which proposed investments contribute to fulfillment of agency mission and goals. The highest-priority investments are to be selected for funding.

If the enterprise is an executive-level agency, after prioritizing and selecting information system investments the IRB forms a portfolio request for Major Investments for review by OMB. If the enterprise is one of several in an executive-level agency, the IRB process is repeated at the agency level, with the agency-level IRB prioritizing and approving Major Investments from across its enterprises to form an agency-wide investment portfolio request for review by OMB.

2.3 Requirements versus Reality: The Need for Improvement

While the capital budgeting process for federal information system security investments is fairly well established in principle, the complexity of the process makes investments difficult to justify, much less optimize. These complexities include the fact that information system security investments proposed to executive agencies for funding are a small, often-overlooked part of the overall investment request for the information system. Another complicating factor relates to the highly uneven levels of maturity in managing resources for information system security investments across enterprises and agencies. Larger agencies may have capital planning and investment specialists on staff, and consultants available for hire, to help them decipher and navigate the process to ensure their investment proposals are highly rated by their superiors. Some have developed customized software that meets their agency-specific needs—and only their needs—for this purpose. Information system security investment needs for the smaller agencies may not be as large in dollar value, but they may be as urgent as those of larger agencies.

The time dimension further complicates decision-making. As the likelihood and magnitude of threats to the federal information infrastructure continue to evolve, and administrations come and go, OMB policy and NIST guidance—which determine federal information system security priorities—are sure to change. Thus, an effective decision-making approach will be one that accommodates the fluid nature of that environment.

These complexities demand a theoretically sound, practical, and flexible approach to budgeting for information system security at all stages of the process, supporting decisions made at the system, enterprise, and executive levels. Otherwise, inefficient allocation of scarce budgetary resources may result. A promising approach possessing all of these attributes—theoretical soundness, practicality, and flexibility—is the subject of the next chapter.

3 The Analytic Hierarchy Process[2]

3.1 Structure of the Analytic Hierarchy Process

The Analytic Hierarchy Process (AHP) was developed in the early 1970's by Thomas L. Saaty of the Wharton School at the University of Pennsylvania[3] and has since come into the mainstream of conventional multiattribute decision analysis. It constitutes a comprehensive method of evaluation to support decisions for which both quantitative and qualitative attributes are relevant. The AHP is described in detail in ASTM Standard E 1765-02, *Standard Practice for Applying Analytic Hierarchy Process (AHP) to Multiattribute Decision Analysis of Investments Related to Buildings and Building Systems.*[4]

The following is a description of the structure and application of the AHP; it is given to explain the theoretical foundation for a software tool that will be developed to support information security investment decisions. This tool would automate the ranking procedure described and illustrated in this chapter. Readers who are familiar with the method may want to go directly to Chapters 4 and 5, which respectively relate the AHP to information system security and apply it through an illustrative case example.

The AHP is a relatively straightforward approach for combining "apples and oranges" in support of resource allocation decisions. A resource allocation decision for managing federal information system security investments includes attributes that are not all measurable in the same units, may not be measurable at all, or cannot be expressed in dollars. The AHP approach allows both financial and non-financial attributes to be taken into account in the decision-making process and combines their impacts into a single measure of desirability for the investment alternatives considered.

The AHP has four major features: (1) It decomposes a complex problem into its constituent elements and orders them into a "hierarchy", or classification system; (2) it uses pairwise comparisons to establish priorities among elements in each level of the hierarchy: (3) it provides a measurement theory to estimate the relative weights of the elements; and (4) it aggregates the relative weights to derive a single overall rating for each decision alternative.

3.1.1 The Hierarchy

The AHP decomposes the factors of a complex decision problem into groups according to properties they have in common and arranges these groups in a hierarchical fashion. Each level of the hierarchy consists of a manageable number of elements (Saaty suggests a maximum of

---

[2] This chapter is adapted from S. K. Fuller, *Risk Exposure and Risk Attitude of Homeowners in Fire Protection Investment Decisions,* NISTIR 89-4212 (Gaithersburg, MD: National Institute of Standards and Technology, 1989).
[3] T. L. Saaty, *The Analytic Hierarchy Process* (New York, NY: McGraw-Hill, 1980).
[4] ASTM International, "Standard Practice for Applying Analytic Hierarchy Process (AHP) to Multiattribute Decision Analysis of Investments Related to Buildings and Building Systems," E 1765-02, *ASTM Standards on Building Economics,* 5th edition (West Conshohocken, PA, 2002).

nine, but this is not a necessary condition), which again may be decomposed into another set of elements at the next lower level. The process continues from the overall goal of a problem down to specific criteria, that is, from the more general (and sometimes more uncertain) to the more particular and definite. The bottom level of a hierarchy usually contains the alternatives from which the choice is to be made.

Using an information system security example, the goal, "Risk-Based Information System Security," appears at the top tier of the hierarchy in Figure 3.1. The next lower level lists factors contributing to the goal, such as "Confidentiality," "Integrity," "Availability." These in turn serve as criteria for selecting among investment alternatives A, B, and C.[5]

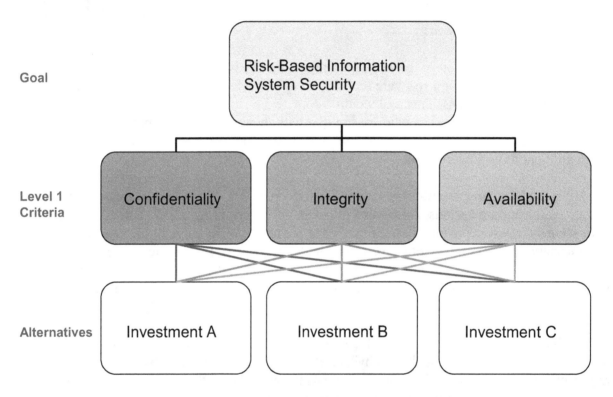

Figure 3.1   Example of an AHP Hierarchy

For more complex decisions, the hierarchy may have more levels and a greater number of criteria. And even though a hierarchy has a vertical stratification, it need not be complete, that is, an element at a higher level need not function as a criterion for all the elements in the lower level. The hierarchy can be partitioned into sub-hierarchies sharing only a common topmost element. (Figure 4.1 shows an example of one such hierarchy.)

This feature of being able to arrange the elements of a complex selection process into partial hierarchies and sub-hierarchies makes the AHP flexible and allows it to be tailored to an enterprise's level of investment management maturity. A low level of investment management maturity will require only a few criteria and sub-criteria to be ordered and evaluated with respect

---

[5] The criteria of confidentiality, integrity and availability are being used to illustrate the method. A more complex set of criteria, yet to be defined, is required for accurately selecting investment alternatives.

to an overall goal, whereas at a high level of investment management maturity there may be multiple levels, criteria, and sub-criteria.

The use of the hierarchical structure is based on the precept that hierarchical classification is a natural method of the human mind to order experience, observation, and information. A hierarchy, through the interaction of the various levels, makes it easier to understand how a decision affects the overall goal at the highest level; the effect of a multitude of unordered facts is much more difficult to grasp. The mere ordering of complex data into a flexible and readily identifiable structure makes it easier for decision-makers who come from different entities within a department or an enterprise to collaborate with one another on, for example, the allocation of a common budget, such as an enterprise information system budget.

Like the structuring of a problem by any other method, the design of an analytic hierarchy requires the input of individuals knowledgeable about the problem in question. What factors are relevant, how they should be grouped, and in which levels, are issues that need to be resolved. In doing so, the information necessary for sound decision-making is generated and organized. A relatively simple problem, such as the one in Figure 3.1, may require only the input of one decision-maker who uses the appropriate sources of information. A more complex problem may require a decision-maker's consultation with other experts familiar with the problem. Or, information from published documents, such as the NIST 800 series, may be used directly to design an analytic hierarchy.[6] If there are several parties involved but only a single decision-maker, the decision-maker may consult with the other parties and reflect their preferences when applying the model. If there are several decision-makers, each one of them may apply the AHP to rank the alternative solutions; these rankings can then be consolidated by taking simple or weighted averages.

3.1.2 The Pairwise Comparisons

In the absence of quantitative data indicating the importance or preference of one element over another at a given level, a procedure of paired comparisons may be used. Each pair of criteria is compared with respect to each element in the level above to which they both contribute. For example, Investment A in Figure 3.1 may be compared with Investments B or C, with respect to its relative contribution to confidentiality, integrity, and availability, of information. The decision-maker can also assign importance weights or preference ratings directly to the elements of a level. For example, instead of a series of pairwise comparisons of the investment alternatives with respect to confidentiality, integrity, and availability, the decision-maker could directly assign numeric ratings to these alternatives if quantitative data exist.

When making pairwise comparisons, in addition to determining the preference of one element over another, the decision-maker expresses the intensity of that preference. Table 3.1 shows an "intensity of importance" scale developed by Saaty.[7] Saaty has demonstrated that only the whole numbers 1 to 9 are needed to indicate the intensity of preference, with a 1 meaning that the two items being compared are of equal importance and a 9 meaning the first item is extremely more

---

[6] NIST guidance is given in the 800 series of special publications on information system security published by the National Institute of Standards and Technology, Gaithersburg, MD.
[7] T. L. Saaty, *Decision Making for Leaders* (Gelmont, CA: Lifetime Learning Publications, 1982).

important than the second. Table 3.1 shows how the AHP translates verbal judgments ranging from "equal importance" to "extreme importance" into intensity scores of 1, 3, 5, 7, or 9, with 2, 4, 6, and 8 as intermediate values between adjacent judgments.

Table 3.1   Definitions of Pairwise Comparison Judgment Scale

Intensity of Importance	Definition	Explanation
1	Equal importance of elements	Two elements contribute equally to the higher-level element
3	Moderate importance of one element over another	Experience and judgment slightly favor one element over another
5	Strong importance of one element over another	Experience and judgment strongly favor one element over another
7	Very strong importance of one element over another	An element is strongly favored and its dominance is demonstrated in practice
9	Extreme importance of one element over another	The evidence favoring one element over another is of the highest possible order of affirmation
2, 4, 6, & 8	Intermediate values between two adjacent judgments	Used when compromise is needed between two judgments
Reciprocals	If element i has one of the above numbers assigned to it when compared with element j, then j has the reciprocal value when compared with i.	

Source: S. I. Gass, *Decision Making, Models and Algorithms* (New York, NY: John Wiley & Sons, 1985), chapter 24, p. 357.

When comparing elements in the AHP hierarchy, one needs to frame questions so they elicit the decision-maker's view of the importance (or preference) of one element over another. For example, at the topmost tier of the hierarchy in Figure 3.1, one might ask the following: "With respect to risk-based information system security, confidentiality is how much more important than availability?" A value of 3 means that the decision-maker considers the criterion of confidentiality to be moderately more important than the criterion of availability with respect to the goal of risk-based information system security. The reciprocal comparison of availability and confidentiality receives a value of 1/3. When compared with itself, each element has equal importance and gets a value of 1.

Note that it is important to ask the question in such a way that the scalar system is maintained. The smaller of two elements being compared is considered to be the unit and the larger one is assessed to be so many times more than it, using the intensity of feeling and translating it to the numeric intensity value. But it is not necessary that the comparisons be mutually "consistent" in the strict sense of "transitivity."[8] For example, the scale value of 9 should remain approximately three times as favorable as the scale value of 3, but if confidentiality is judged twice as important as integrity, and integrity three times as important as availability, then the final ranking is not influenced much if confidentiality is not strictly six times as important as availability. That there is slight inconsistency in judgments is a realistic assumption to make and one that can be accommodated by the AHP.[9] Lack of consistency can have many sources, as for instance, a different frame of reference or differing opinions.[10]

3.1.3 Aggregation of Relative Weights and Ratings

The solution technique of the AHP takes as inputs the values generated by the pairwise comparisons and produces as outputs the relative weights of the hierarchy elements. To help decide which investment to select, an overall rating of the alternatives is necessary, that is, the results from all tiers of the hierarchy have to be aggregated. To aggregate the relative weights and preference ratings – whether developed through pairwise comparison or direct use of quantitative data – they are "synthesized" by factoring the influence of the preceding levels into the decision. The result is an overall ranking, based on the calculated priorities, of the investment alternatives in the lowest tier of the hierarchy.

Section A.2 in Appendix A describes how the priorities of the decision elements are generated and aggregated. Section A.3 briefly describes the theoretical basis of the pairwise comparison method, including the relationship between the consistency of the pairwise comparisons and the reliability of the resulting priorities.

3.2 Advantages and Limitations of the AHP

The AHP method has been used for applications as diverse as energy policy formulation, marketing, accounting and auditing, subjective probability estimation, evaluation of expert systems, and selection of microcomputers. These applications seem unrelated, but they share a set of common features. All involve a rating of decision alternatives for evaluation, selection, and prediction.

3.2.1 Limitations

One criticism raised about the AHP concerns the requirement to explicitly state and incorporate subjective judgments. This requirement is rejected by some members of the operations research and management science communities, who are reluctant to adopt a method that does not claim

---

[8] Saaty, 1980.
[9] See discussion of consistency in Section 3.2.2
[10] J. M. Hihn, and C. R. Johnson, "Evaluation Techniques for Paired Ratio-Comparison Matrices in a Hierarchical Decision Model," in *Measurement in Economics*, ed. W. Eichhorn (Heidelberg, Germany: 1988).

to be purely "objective." However, recent trends in the philosophy of science support the view that subjectivity plays a role in scientific analysis and that there is a linkage between scientific methods, cognition, and beliefs.[11] All preference-eliciting methods have to deal with the problem of ambiguity. The AHP allows decision-makers to comprehend the issue at hand and use its structure to meaningfully address it.

Saaty (1980) and other researchers do not insist that the AHP is the only valid method to analyze decision problems or that it is applicable to all problems. But after taking its assumptions and limitations into account, they offer it as one among several aids to decision-making for problems that include qualitative or intuitive judgments or are too unstructured for traditional techniques.

3.2.2 Advantages

The AHP is well suited to facilitate and encourage cost-efficient compliance with information security requirements without overly burdening decision-makers with the demanding techniques and data requirements needed for more rigorous assessments. There are many benefits to the federal community from adopting an AHP-based resource allocation model for its information system budgetary requests. The AHP provides the needed structure and mathematical foundation to evaluate subjective information in a fair and systematic manner. It accomplishes this by arranging investment criteria, sub-criteria, scales of intensity, and alternatives in such a way that decision-makers can logically and consistently evaluate all of the alternatives in a complex decision problem. Furthermore, it presents decision-makers with a single combined performance score for each alternative that can be used to rank-order the alternatives. The AHP is more desirable than other processes using qualitative judgments because it not only enables a direct rank ordering of investment alternatives but an actual measurement of the relative *degree* to which alternatives satisfy the investment goal. Hence, the results carry more meaning and value to support resource allocation. Also, the AHP, which is standardized in ASTM Standard Practice E 1765-02, helps meet overarching OMB requirements that agencies reduce reliance on government-unique standards and benefit from the expertise of the private sector.[12] Finally, the AHP process can be automated through software, which will greatly facilitate its application. All told, the AHP approach would enable system owners to better, and more efficiently, justify their budget requests. Indeed, the AHP is used by the U.S. Department of Veteran's Affairs to develop a completely integrated capital investment portfolio, helping them become the first organization in the federal government to successfully integrate their resource allocation process.[13]

---

[11] T. Harker and L. Vargas, "The Theory of Ratio Scale Estimation: Saaty's Analytic Hierarchy Process," *Management Science* 33 (1987): 11.

[12] U.S. Office of Management and Budget, *Federal Participation in the Development and Use of Voluntary Consensus Standards and in Conformity Assessment Activities,* OMB Circular A-119 (Washington, D.C: February 1998).

[13] *VA Capital Investment Methodology Guide: FY 2005* (Draft), available at http://www.va.gov/oaem/FY2005_Guide/FY2005_Capital_Investment_Guide.asp.

4 The AHP Applied to Federal Information System Security

A cost-effective, risk-based approach for integrating security requirements into the information system capital planning process must be rigorous in concept, but straightforward to apply. It is not designed to replace managerial judgment but rather structured for management to make more transparent, consistent, and economically defensible decisions. It must also be amenable to the existing framework for securing federal information system resources established by legislative mandates as well as NIST guidance. Finally, an effective approach for integrating security requirements into the information system capital planning process must be systematic but at the same time flexible enough to seamlessly accommodate rapidly changing information security requirements. As demonstrated in the previous chapter, the AHP is just such an approach. This chapter illustrates how the AHP could be applied to the capital planning process for information security.

As noted in the previous chapter, in the context of the AHP, the set of quantitative and qualitative characteristics, which together contribute to the investment goal, are referred to as criteria. For complex decision problems the criteria are divided into their contributing elements, referred to as sub-criteria. An AHP resource allocation model then rates investment alternatives against criteria and sub-criteria through use of scales of intensity, or yardsticks. An AHP resource allocation model consists of the following elements structured into a hierarchy:

- Investment goal;
- Investment criteria, known as Level 1 Criteria, contributing to attainment of the investment goal;
- Investment sub-criteria, known as Level 2 Criteria, contributing to attainment of the Level 1 Criteria;
- Investment alternatives; and
- Scales of intensity for rating investment alternatives against sub-criteria and/or criteria.

Figure 4.1 displays an AHP hierarchy that can serve as a tentative framework for organizing the investment selection process for information system security. The goal of the process is cost-effective, risk-based information system security. Contributing to this goal are four basic investment criteria:

1. Agency goals (degree to which investment aligns with agency missions and business processes).
2. Cost-effective security.
3. Identified material weaknesses and Plan of Action and Milestones (POA&M) (significant deficiencies found in the course of security assessments for which immediate or near-immediate corrective action must be taken, as detailed in POA&M.
4. Risk-based security.[14]

---

[14] These four investment criteria are explained and justified in more detail in section 5.2.2.

13

The investment alternatives are evaluated directly with respect to the first three criteria using quantitative data such as estimated investment costs, where available, and the pairwise comparison method described in Section 3.1.2 otherwise. The risk-based criterion is further specified as Level 2 Criteria: system confidentiality, integrity, and availability. In the absence of quantitative data, the pairwise comparison method will also be used to assess how well the alternatives satisfy each Level 2 Criterion.

For AHP applications at the system and enterprise architecture levels, where the best security investment from among a number of alternatives is chosen, the importance weights for the Level 2 Criteria can default to values reflecting the FIPS-199 [15] security impact levels of Low, Moderate or High, which indicate the extent of the adverse effect a security event would have on each Level 2 Criterion. Weights for the three FIPS-199 ratings can be established through pairwise comparison by the enterprise's IRB and be suggested for use by system owners proposing security investments for funding. (If for any reason the system owner believes use of a different set of weights to be more appropriate, that system owner would be required to document and justify the new weight set as part of the proposal package.) Similarly, the IRB can use the pairwise comparison process to fix the Level 1 weights—indicating the relative importance of agency goals, cost-effective information system security, identified material weaknesses and POA&M, and risk-based computer security—to be applied throughout the enterprise.

Once the best system- and enterprise-level security investments have been identified by the system owner, they are forwarded for consideration by the IRB. The IRB is charged with selecting the highest-priority investment from among those proposed for funding. To support this process, each investment proposal can be required to include documentation of its AHP evaluation, so that the IRB can readily rank the proposed investments from throughout the enterprise on the basis of their overall AHP ratings, selecting investments in rank order until the security budget is exhausted.

---

[15] FIPS 199, *Standards for Security Categorization of Federal Information and Information Systems,* February 2004.

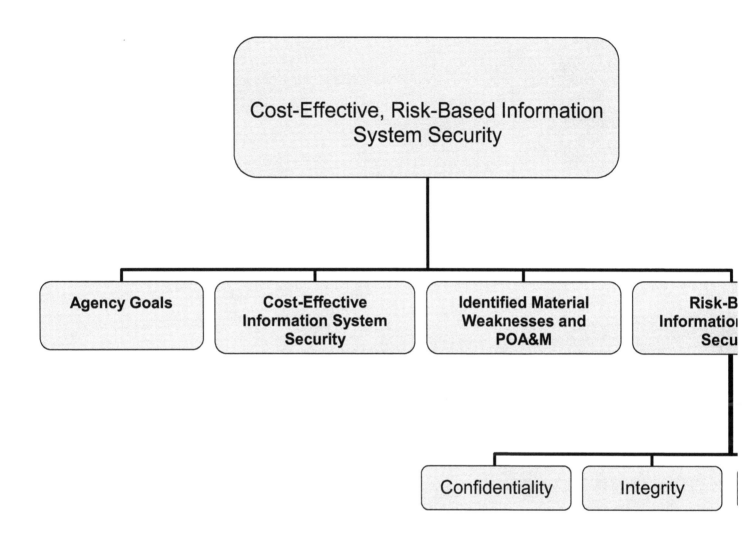

Figure 4.1 AHP Hierarchy for Security Investment Selection

15

5 The AHP Applied to Federal Information System Security: A Case Study

5.1 Defining the Case Study

5.1.1 Introduction

The case study described in this chapter is intended to illustrate how the AHP can be used by resource managers of an enterprise to select information system security investments that are cost-effective, given the likelihood and magnitude of threats to its information infrastructure.

It is assumed that the decision-makers are the information system owners of a federal enterprise who have access to information that allows them to evaluate, in a quantitative or qualitative way, the security requirements of new systems and the weaknesses of existing systems. In the case of numeric data the decision-makers' objectivity is taken for granted; in the case of qualitative data related to information security, they are considered "experts" in their field so that the information they have available will cause their judgments to reflect objective facts. Investment criteria outside their realm of expertise (e.g., those related to overall agency goals) will be weighted by the IRB and required for use by information system owners throughout the enterprise.

In the present illustrative application of the AHP, information needed to define the criteria, sub-criteria and alternatives has been obtained from experts within a federal enterprise and is based on a representative investment project.

5.1.2 Project Description

The project used to illustrate the AHP has as its goal to develop a cost-effective and secure application for an agency program that receives from outside organizations proprietary information related to proposals for a national award. The award proposals are evaluated by teams of outside examiners within a specific time frame. The web site needs to ensure that examiners and inside agency staff can upload and download files without compromising the confidentiality, integrity, and availability of the information that is exchanged. The application includes an administrative module for staff to manage accounts.

In this case study it is assumed that agency program managers and its Chief Information Officer (CIO) were involved in the design of the application from its beginning stages. All informational requirements regarding capital asset planning and alternatives analysis have been met. Three investment alternatives, Investments A, B and C, have been developed to meet the security needs of the application. The required security controls, even though an integral part of the application design, are clearly spelled out and priced separately.

The application is hosted on the agency's private network and is categorized as an application of moderate impact according to FIPS 199. It is being developed with somewhat higher security needs in mind than the applications that are hosted on the agency's outside public network, where no sensitive information may reside.

The following security practices need to be addressed, some of which are already included in the standard security measures in place for other public-facing applications within the agency:

Antivirus Management
Patch Monitoring, Patch Application, and Patch Verification
Certification and Accreditation Procedures
Systems Administration Access
Systems Software and Hardware Inventory Process
System Monitoring

The three proposed investment alternatives, Investments A, B and C, add protection against vulnerabilities specific to the proposal evaluation process during which outside teams of reviewers and inside support monitors and administrators have to interact in stages and have to have access to partly public and partly sensitive information.

5.2 AHP Model for Case Study

It is assumed for this case study that the agency has a process in place for managing its information security investments but has limited quantitative data for evaluating them. The AHP application demonstrates how a system owner can rate the different investment options, depending on their particular contributions to agency goals, cost-effectiveness, risk mitigation, or other criteria considered important, but for which data are not necessarily available in numeric form.

5.2.1 Construction of Hierarchy

Figure 5.1 shows the evaluation hierarchy for the project in this case example. The goal for the system owner is to identify the "best" investment for ensuring Cost-effective, Risk-based Information System Security for the project, given agency-wide goals, budget constraints, and the specific threats faced by the system. The circumstances that define these aspects are captured in Level 1 by the criteria *Agency Goals, Cost-effective Information System Security, Identified Material Weaknesses and POA&M,* and *Risk-based Information System Security.*

The criterion *Risk-based Information System Security* is broken down into sub-criteria in Level 2 to allow for an additional level of detail. The sub-criteria *Confidentiality, Integrity, Availability* represent the objectives that contribute to ensuring *Risk-based Information System Security* in the level above.

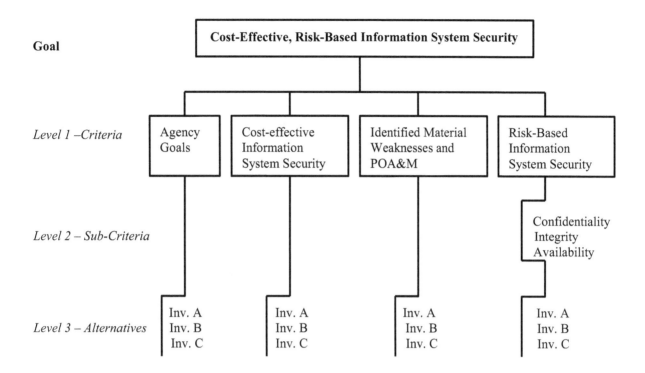

Figure 5.1   AHP Hierarchy for Case Study

Level 3 contains the investment alternatives, *Investments A, B and C,* which will be evaluated with respect to the criteria in the levels directly above. All judgments at the various levels of the hierarchy will be made based on quantitative or qualitative data.

5.2.2 Discussion of Criteria, Sub-criteria, and Alternatives

A discussion of criteria, sub-criteria, and alternatives serves several interrelated purposes: (1) to define them in a way that captures all relevant aspects of the decision problem; (2) to provide the background information needed to make judgments; (3) to clarify in what way non-quantitative information is relevant to making decisions about investments in information system security; and (4) to relate the data provided by agency experts to the application of the AHP.

The information considered relevant to the goal of *Cost-effective, Risk-based Information System Security* is presented and discussed below under headings corresponding to the hierarchy elements shown in Figure 5.1.

OVERALL GOAL: COST-EFFECTIVE, RISK-BASED INFORMATION SYSTEM SECURITY

The relative importance, with respect to the overall goal, of each of the Level 1 criteria (i.e., *Agency Goals, Cost-effective Information System Security, Identified Material Weaknesses and POA&M* and *Risk-based Information System Security*) may be determined by the agency management or the IRB and be required for use by all system owners seeking funds for security-related information system investments.

CRITERIA

AGENCY GOALS (Level 1 Criterion)

Because the selection of appropriate security measures inherently affects an agency's ability to perform its mission and to achieve specific program outcomes, the selection process cannot be treated as only a technical function carried out by the information system experts who operate and manage information systems, but must be considered an essential management function as well. Some of the associated systems or projects may have significant program or policy implications and high executive visibility and hence require special management attention that needs to be taken into account in the decision-making process. As such, the investment alternatives have to be evaluated with respect to their contributions to agency missions and business needs within the framework of the capital planning and investment control process. For the case example, the agency goal to be supported by the proposed investment is management of a high-visibility national award program.

Level 3 Alternatives: It has been determined that all three of the investment alternatives contribute in equal measure to *Agency Goals*.

COST-EFFECTIVE INFORMATION SYSTEM SECURITY (Level 1 Criterion)

Because funding is limited, investments in information system security need to meet the prescribed performance requirements at the lowest possible cost and with a rate of return equal to or higher than for alternate uses of funding. The criterion *Cost-effective Information System Security* makes it possible to include in the decision-making the differing contributions of the investment alternatives towards this criterion.

Level 3 Alternatives: All three investment alternatives address the overall security needs of the application, but their dollar costs vary because of the differing combinations of tools included in each alternative. The investment costs include initial costs as well as future costs such as estimated licensing fees and maintenance costs over a period of 10 years.

Investment A – $790,000
Investment B – $850,000
Investment C – $820,000

Investments A, B, and *C* are ranked with respect to *Cost-effective Information System Security* by directly calculating pairwise ratios from their dollar costs.

IDENTIFIED MATERIAL WEAKNESSES AND POA&M (Level 1 Criterion)

In the course of security assessments, information system owners, enterprise or agency managers, departmental Inspectors General, or the U.S. Government Accountability Office (GAO), may identify a significant deficiency in an agency's overall information systems security program or management control structure, or within one or more information systems. This deficiency is to be reported as a "material weakness" and immediate or near-immediate corrective action must be taken, as detailed in the POA&M.

Level 3 Alternatives: One of the weaknesses identified for the enterprise's information system architecture is the existence of a number of autonomous systems that are difficult to integrate into the general security practices in place throughout the enterprise. All three investment alternatives, *Investments A, B, and C*, address this identified weakness by supporting, albeit at various levels, a centralized network infrastructure and by employing technologies that can be implemented centrally throughout the enterprise.

RISK-BASED INFORMATION SYSTEM SECURITY (Level 1 Criterion)

Through the mandatory Certification and Accreditation (C&A) process, the impact levels for the information system with respect to the three security goals *Confidentiality, Integrity, and Availability* are expressed as Low, Moderate, or High according to FIPS 199. Within this context, the system and information owners can qualitatively judge to what extent the proposed investments contribute to meet the three security goals of confidentiality, integrity, and availability. In the AHP hierarchy, therefore, the criterion *Risk-Based Information System Security* is further described in terms of these three security goals.

CONFIDENTIALITY (Level 2 Sub-criterion)

System and data confidentiality refers to the protection of information from unauthorized disclosure. Unauthorized, unanticipated, or unintentional disclosure could result in loss of public confidence, embarrassment, or legal action against the organization.

INTEGRITY (Level 2 Sub-criterion)

System and data integrity refers to the requirement that information be protected from improper modification. Integrity is lost if unauthorized changes are made to the data or information system by either intentional or accidental acts. Violation of integrity may be the first step in a successful attack against system availability or confidentiality.

AVAILABILITY (Level 2 Sub-criterion)

If a mission-critical information system is unavailable to its end users, the organization's mission may be affected. Loss of system functionality and operational effectiveness may impede the end-users performance of their functions in supporting the organization's mission.

Level 3 Alternatives: Due to the particular combinations of tools and security measures, *Investment A* is slightly more conducive to ensuring confidentiality, *Investment B* to ensuring integrity and *Investment C* to ensuring availability of data.

ALTERNATIVES – Level 3

INVESTMENT A: ($790,000)

- **Network Vulnerability Analysis Tools:** The agency uses two COTS (commercial off-the-shelf) vulnerability analysis tools. One is a closed-source vulnerability scanner that runs on a variety of platforms. The other vulnerability scanner allows scanning policies to be customized and comes with 20 standard scanning policies. *Investment A* adds an open-source penetration testing platform for developing, testing, and using exploit code, which will be integrated into the scanning tools the agency is already using.
- **Encryption Tools:** The sensitivity of the data requires the encryption of the database as well as the encryption of data in transit. An encryption tool already in use at the agency will be used to encrypt files at rest and in transit.
-

INVESTMENT B: ($850,000)

- **Scanning and Enumeration Tools:** *Investment B* adds an open-source command line tool that is used to craft packets with the option to set various flags in the packet header. It is used to audit firewalls. It will be combined with an existing command line tool that creates network connections and with a large-network port scanner that determines, for example, what hosts, services, operating systems, and packet filters/firewalls are in use on the network.
- **Log File Analysis and Monitoring Tools:** A new log file analyzer for Web servers is added and integrated into the existing log file analysis and monitoring tools. The analyzer examines log files and produces a comprehensive array of reports that show patterns in usage and potential intrusion attempts by robots, worms, search engines, keywords, and keyphrases.

INVESTMENT C: ($820,000)

- **Web Vulnerability Analysis Tools:** *Investment C* adds an open-source command line vulnerability web scanner that will be used as a supplementary tool to existing scanners that perform tests against web servers for vulnerabilities. For network functionality the additional scanner is based on a perl module geared to http testing. The scanner relies on a regularly updated database for vulnerability scanning and also supports user-defined checks.
- **Patch Management Tools:** These tools automate the process of keeping machines updated with the latest operating systems and application updates. *Investment C* increases automation to cover every operating system on the private network within the CIO's area of responsibility.

5.2.3 Pairwise Comparisons

5.2.3.1 Level 1 Comparisons – Criteria

Table 5.1 presents the first set of pairwise comparisons in Level 1 of the hierarchy and the priorities calculated from them.[16] Recall that pairwise comparisons are made on the basis of verbal comparisons as defined in Chapter 3, Table 3.1, and translated into their associated "intensity of importance" scores for entry in the judgment matrices. For example, when comparing *Agency Goals* relative to the other criteria, the IRB made the judgment that *Agency Goals* are moderately more important than *Cost-effective Information System Security* and *Risk-Based System Security* but that *Identified Material Weaknesses and POA&M* items, which require immediate or near-immediate corrective action, were equally as important as *Agency Goals*, strongly more important than *Cost-effective Information System Security* and very strongly more important than *Risk-Based Information System Security*. *Cost-effective Information System Security* was judged moderately more important than *Risk-Based Information System Security*.

Table 5.1 Judgment Matrix - Level 1

Cost-effective Risk-based Information System Security	Agency Goals	Cost-eff. Info. Sys. Security	Ident. Material Weakness	Risk-based Info. Sys. Security	Priorities
Agency Goals	1	3	1	3	0.33
Cost-effective Info. Sys. Security		1	1/5	3	0.13
Identified Material Weaknesses and POA&M			1	7	0.47
Risk-based Info. Sys. Security				1	0.07
Consistency Ratio: 0.06					1.00

The criterion *Identified Material Weaknesses and POA&M* receives the highest priority (0.47) relative to the other criteria. This is intuitively to be expected since a material weakness, as described in the POA&M, by definition, significantly restricts the capability of the agency to carry out its mission. According to the Federal Information Security Management Act Section 3544(c)(3), immediate or near-immediate action must be taken; this urgency is accounted for in the ranking of the investment alternatives.

Agency Goals has the second highest priority (0.33), reflecting the need to ensure that the agency's capability of fulfilling its mission is not impeded by excessive layers of protection

---

[16] Section A.1 in Appendix A explains the method of calculating priorities; Sub-section A3.2 treats the derivation of the consistency ratio.

against potential security breaches. *Cost-effective Information System Security* has a higher priority (0.13) than *Risk-Based Information System Security* (0.07), reflecting the reality that funding constraints make it impossible to ensure absolute security, requiring agencies to accept a certain level of vulnerability in some instances.

The consistency ratio for the Table 5.1 judgment matrix was calculated as 0.06 according to the method described in Appendix A, Section A.3.2. It is below 0.10 and thus within the acceptable range required by the AHP methodology.

5.2.3.2   Level 2 Comparisons - Sub-criteria

Table 5.2 presents the set of comparisons in Level 2 of the hierarchy. In Level 2 are the sub-criteria for *Risk-Based Information System Security,* namely *Confidentiality*, *Integrity*, and *Availability*. The system's FIPS-199-assigned level of impact (Low, Moderate, or High) with respect to each sub-criterion forms the basis of the judgments. For this system, where proprietary information coming from outside firms is reviewed, the FIPS 199 process assigned the following impact levels: *Confidentiality*—High, *Integrity*—Moderate, and *Availability*—Low. The IRB has translated these impact levels into the following pairwise comparisons: With respect to *Risk-Based Information System Security,* the subcriterion *Confidentiality* is moderately to strongly more important than *Integrity* and strongly more important than *Availability*. *Integrity* is judged moderately more important than *Availability*.

Table 5.2   Judgment Matrix - Level 2

Risk-based Information System Security	Confidentiality	Integrity	Availability	Priorities
Confidentiality	1	4	5	0.68
Integrity		1	2	0.20
Availability			1	0.12
Consistency Ratio: 0.02				1.00

The relative importance of each risk-based information system security criterion is reflected in the calculated priorities of 0.68 for *Confidentiality*, 0.20 for *Integrity* and 0.12 for *Availability* of the data and systems for which the investments are being considered.

The consistency ratio for this matrix was estimated to be 0.02, indicating a high level of consistency of judgments.

5.2.3.3   Level 3 Comparisons - Alternatives

In Level 3 of the hierarchy, the decision-maker evaluates the information system security technologies available. He or she compares *Investments A, B* and *C* pairwise with each other with respect to each one of the criteria or sub-criteria in the preceding level. For investment costs numerical values are available, so that the priorities can be calculated directly from the dollar amounts. For the remaining criteria and sub-criteria in the hierarchy numerical data for the investment alternatives are not available and so the judgment matrices are again generated using the definitions of the verbal judgments in Table 3.1 of Chapter 3.

Table 5.3 shows the priorities calculated for the investment alternatives. For example, the decision-maker finds that the alternative investments contribute equally to *Agency Goals*. Hence the alternatives are ranked equally, with priorities of 0.33 for each.

For *Cost-effective Information System Security*, the investment priorities can be calculated directly from the normalized ratios of the estimated dollar costs, namely $790,000 for *Investment A*, $850,000 *for Investment B*, and $820,000 for *Investment C*. For *Investment A*, the priority is 0.35 ($=1/850/[1/850 + 1/790 + 1/820]$). Given that *Investment A* has the lowest cost, it scores highest in cost effectiveness, followed by *Investment C* and *Investment B*.

For *Identified Material Weaknesses and POA&M,* all three investment alternatives were designed to reduce vulnerabilities by focusing on technologies that can be implemented centrally and promote the integration of security practices into the general information system architecture. *Investment B* is moderately to strongly preferred to *Investment A* and moderately preferred to *Investment C* with respect to this criterion by replacing, in addition, a portion of the legacy equipment that in part causes the identified vulnerabilities. The relative importance of each of the investments in *Identified Material Weaknesses and POA&M* is reflected in the priorities of 0.22 for *Investment A*, 0.63 for *Investment B*, and 0.15 for *Investment C*.

The priorities for each of the investment alternatives with respect to *Confidentiality, Integrity, and Availability* show that *Investment A*, with a priority of 0.67, contributes more to enhancing *Confidentiality* than *B* and *C*; *Investment B*, with a priority of 0.64, contributes more to enhancing *Integrity* than *A* and *C*; and *Investment C*, with a priority of 0.65, contributes more to enhancing *Availability* than *A* and *B*.

The consistency ratios of the judgment matrices of Table 5.3 are all within the acceptable range of less than 10 %.

Table 5.3. Judgments and Estimated Priorities — Investment Alternatives

Agency Goals (0.33)	A	B	C	Priorities
Investment A				0.33
Investment B	All investment alternatives are			0.33
Investment C	contributing equally to goal			0.33
	Consistency Ratio = 0.0			1.00
Cost-eff. Info. Sys. Security (0.13)	A	B	C	Priorities
Investment A				0.35
Investment B	Priorities calculated numerically			0.32
Investment C				0.33
	Consistency Ratio: 0.0			1.00
Identified Material Weaknesses (0.47)	A	B	C	Priorities
Investment A	1	1/4	2	0.22
Investment B	4	1	3	0.63
Investment C	1/2	1/3	1	0.15
	Consistency Ratio: 0.09			1.00
Risk-Based Info. Sys. Security (0.068)	A	B	C	
Confidentiality (0.68)				Priorities
Inv.A	1	5	4	0.67
Inv.B	1/5	1	1/3	0.10
Inv.C	1/4	3	1	0.23
	Consistency Ratio: 0.08			1.00
Integrity (0.20)	A	B	C	Priorities
Inv.A	1	1/5	1/3	0.10
Inv.B	5	1	3	0.64
Inv.C	3	1/3	1	0.26
	Consistency Ratio: 0.03			1.00
Availability (0.12)	A	B	C	Priorities
Inv.A	1	2	1/3	0.23
Inv.B	1/2	1	1/5	0.12
Inv.C	3	5	1	0.65
	Consistency Ratio: 0.04			1.00

5.2.4 Ranking

For an overall ranking of the investment alternatives, the priorities of criteria, sub-criteria and investment alternatives from each level of the hierarchy are aggregated and "synthesized" to include the results of the preceding levels. The tally of this synthesis is shown in Table 5.4.

The final priorities are summed for each investment alternative to arrive at an overall ranking, as shown in Table 5.5. For example, the global priority for Investment A is calculated as the sum of the intermediate priorities for Investment A in the last column of Table 5.4 (0.1113 + 0.0446 + 0.1025 + 0.0315 + 0.0014 + 0.0018 = 0.2931). The consistency ratio for the entire hierarchy of this case study was calculated as 0.05, a value in the acceptable range.

What these results imply is that the AHP finds *Investment B* to be the best investment for ensuring cost-effective, risk-based information system security for the web site application considered. *Investment A* is ranked second and *Investment C* third. These final composite priorities derived from the AHP combine the information system owner's quantitative and qualitative understanding of a complex problem situation and indicate how the investment alternatives are ordered from most to least favorable. Based on the AHP rankings, the information system owner forwards to the IRB a request for funding *Investment B*.

Once the best security investments have been identified by information system owners from throughout the enterprise and forwarded for consideration by the IRB, the IRB can consistently and efficiently select the highest-priority from among these proposed investments for funding. To support this process, each investment proposal can be required to include documentation of its AHP evaluation, so that the IRB can readily rank the proposed investments from throughout the enterprise on the basis of their overall AHP ratings, selecting investments in rank order until the security budget is exhausted.

Table 5.4 Tally for Synthesis of Priorities for Investment Alternatives

Select Best Investment Alternative for **Cost-effective, Risk-Based Information System Security**		
Level 1 - Criteria	Level 2 - Sub-criteria	Level 3 - Alternatives
Agency Goals = 0.33		Investment A = 0.1113 Investment B = 0.1113 Investment C = 0.1113 **0.3339**
Cost-effective Information System Security = 0.13		Investment A = 0.0446 Investment B = 0.0416 Investment C = 0.0429 **0.1289**
Identified Material Weakness = 0.47		Investment A = 0.1025 Investment B = 0.2953 Investment C = 0.0711 **0.4688**
Risk-Based Information System Security = 0.068	**Confidentiality** = 0.0467	Investment A = 0.0315 Investment B = 0.0047 Investment C = 0.0105 **0.0467**
	Integrity = 0.0137	Investment A = 0.0014 Investment B = 0.0087 Investment C = 0.0036 **0.0137**
	Availability = 0.0080 0.0684	Investment A = 0.0018 Investment B = 0.0009 Investment C = 0.0052 **0.0080** **Total = 1.0000**

Table 5.5   Ranking of Cost-effective, Risk-Based Information System Security Investments

Rank	Alternatives	Priorities
1	Investment B	0.46
2	Investment A	0.29
3	Investment C	0.25

6 Summary and Directions for Further Research

6.1 Summary

This report demonstrates a theoretically sound, practical, and flexible approach for selecting cost-effective strategies to achieve a level of federal information system security commensurate with the degree of vulnerability and magnitude of likely harm. The approach, known as the Analytic Hierarchy Process (AHP), provides the needed structure and mathematical foundation to evaluate subjective information in a fair and systematic manner. It does so by arranging investment criteria and security investment alternatives so decision-makers can logically and consistently evaluate all of the alternatives in a complex decision problem. Furthermore, it presents decision-makers with a single combined performance score for each alternative that can be used to rank-order the investment alternatives. The AHP is more desirable than other processes using qualitative judgments because it not only enables a direct rank ordering of investment alternatives but an actual measurement of the relative *degree* to which alternatives satisfy the investment goal. Because of the measurement, the results carry more meaning and value to support resource allocation.

A case study has illustrated that the AHP is well suited to facilitate and encourage cost-effective compliance with information system security requirements without overly burdening decision-makers with the demanding techniques and data requirements needed for more rigorous assessments. Indeed, the AHP is used by the U.S. Department of Veteran's Affairs to develop completely integrated capital investment portfolios, thus becoming the first organization in the federal government to successfully integrate their resource allocation process.[17] The approach is also used by senior information system executives in the U.S. Department of Housing and Urban Development to help them prioritize over 165 information system projects each year.[18] Finally, the AHP, which is standardized in ASTM Standard Practice E 1765-02, helps meet overarching OMB requirements that agencies reduce reliance on government-unique standards and benefit from the expertise of the private sector.[19]

The AHP has several important benefits: (1) it is well-known and well-reviewed in the literature; (2) it includes an efficient process for user-defined weighting of criteria and sub-criteria; (3) it incorporates hierarchical descriptions of the criteria, sub-criteria, scales of intensity, and alternatives; (4) its use can be facilitated through software; and (5) it has been accepted by ASTM International as a standard practice for investment decision-

---

[17] *VA Capital Investment Methodology Guide: FY 2005* (Draft), available at http://www.va.gov/oaem/FY2005_Guide/FY2005_Capital_Investment_Guide.asp.

[18] For more information on this and other AHP applications, visit http://www.expertchoice.com/customers/successstories.htm.

[19] U.S. Office of Management and Budget, *Federal Participation in the Development and Use of Voluntary Consensus Standards and in Conformity Assessment Activities,* OMB Circular A-119, Washington, D.C., February 1998.

making. All told, the AHP approach enables federal security professionals to better, and more efficiently, justify their budget requests.

6.2 Directions for Further Research

The AHP approach is a viable process, established in an ASTM Standard Method. However, research is needed to develop an industry-approved set of criteria that can be used with the AHP method to accurately select investment alternatives. This report will be used to frame an agenda for a future workshop on what criteria to use in measuring the return on security investments. Once a solid set of criteria is defined that all agencies can implement, follow-on activities, which are described below, can begin.

6.2.1 Step 1. Automate the AHP Approach

Now that the mathematical foundation of the AHP approach has been established and its applicability to federal information system security investment decisions demonstrated, it can be automated in a software program. A software tool would greatly facilitate its application by security professionals and capital budgeting officials by implementing the method without requiring that users be experts in the mathematics of the AHP. The tool should be designed to be flexible for use by decision-makers at all levels throughout an agency, including information system owners, enterprise managers, and agency officials, and should provide the practical, consistent, transparent decision support that is essential for selecting and justifying the most cost-effective information system security investment portfolio. The purpose is to simultaneously simplify and strengthen information system security capital planning by institutionalizing established, repeatable, automated processes that comply with federal policy and guidance.

6.2.2 Step 2. Accommodate Increasing Levels of Investment Management Maturity

A mature, data-rich investment management process should be thought of as a long-term goal rather than an immediate, one-size-fits-all solution. Recent news reports[20] and a series of federal stakeholder interviews convened by NIST and held in February and March 2006 have confirmed that federal agencies vary widely in the maturity of their information system investment management processes. Figure 6.1 shows an Information Technology Investment Management (ITIM) maturity classification system developed by GAO. Most agencies are thought to be at the lowest levels of maturity, Stages 1 or 2. Therefore, the AHP application to federal information system security described and illustrated in this report is tailored to a Stage 2 level of maturity.

---

[20] John Pulley, "Disciplinary Review: Top-notch Investment Review Boards Enforce IT Spending Discipline, but They're Hard to Find," *Federal Computer Week*, May 22, 2006. Available online at http://fcw.com/article94569-05-22-06-Print .

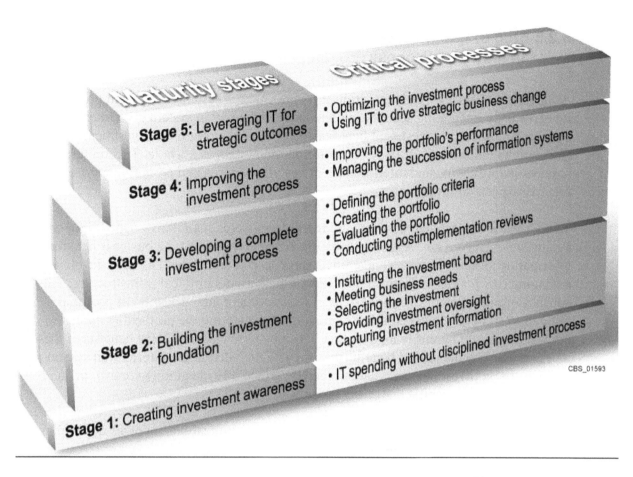

Figure 6.1 IT Investment Management Maturity Model[21]

An AHP framework tailored to Stage 2 enterprises can help them make consistent, transparent resource allocation decisions today while at the same time enabling them to evolve to more mature stages of investment management over time. It can do so by introducing Stage 2 enterprises to a simplified, structured investment prioritization process that can be progressively expanded to accommodate the more rigorous Stage 3 and ultimately Stage 4 levels of decision-making. Over time, AHP decision hierarchies of greater complexity can be constructed and used by agencies at these more advanced stages of ITIM maturity. While the AHP decision hierarchy will be different for each stage of ITIM maturity, the AHP *evaluation process* will remain the same. That is, while hierarchies and data requirements become more complex and quantitative as ITIM maturity evolves, the mathematical foundation for ranking and selecting investments for funding will not change. The idea is to encourage agencies at the early stages of development to begin instituting discipline and rigor in their investment decisions, while at the same time helping them seamlessly evolve to a Stage 5 level of ITIM maturity.

---

[21] Figure 6.1 was adapted by NIST 800-65 from GAO-04-394-G, *Information Technology Investment Management, A Framework for Assessing and Improving Process Maturity*, Version 1.1, March 2004.

31

6.2.3 Step 3. Integrate Security into the Overall Information System Investment Process

A Stage 5 enterprise is ready to optimize its information system investment process. This involves truly integrating security into the larger information system investment context by including security investment benefits and costs in the return-on-investment calculations required by OMB for the information system as a whole. This, in turn, requires identification and monetization of specific benefits and costs flowing from the security aspects of investments.

While security investment cost data are readily available, quantitative benefit—or cost avoidance—data are not. Agencies can monetize and document the business benefits of information system security by adapting a three-step protocol that has been developed for managing risk for cost-effective protection of the nation's physical infrastructure.[22] It consists of the following essential steps: risk assessment, identification of potential mitigation strategies, and economic evaluation. By adapting the protocol to apply to information system security investments, it can be used to quantify the benefits of these investments. The monetized benefits may then be included in the information system-level return on investment calculation, thereby effectively integrating security in the information system capital budgeting process.

Adapting the protocol to information system security applications involves developing a framework of possible damage scenarios, a mechanism supporting development of probability assessments for these scenarios, and a listing of agency-level vulnerabilities. The effort also involves developing a taxonomy of potential impacts from inadequate or excessive information system security (e.g., lost revenue, cost to recover from a security event, productivity losses from excessive security) for consideration by agencies in quantifying losses from alternative damage scenarios. By defining a consistent framework for collection and evaluation of benefit data, an agency, over time, can develop baseline datasets that may be used over and over again in developing benefit estimates for its proposed information system security investments.

Federal information system security professionals juggle budgeting responsibilities along with a wide range of other important duties. They require practical, straightforward tools to support their budget requests and that use established, repeatable processes consistent with federal policy and guidance. By implementing—and automating—the AHP approach to support system-, enterprise-, and agency-level decisions, and by supporting quantification of security benefits only for those limited number of requests that are forwarded to OMB for funding, stakeholder needs will be addressed. As a result, federal information system security professionals can be proactive, rather than reactive, in fulfilling their budgeting responsibilities and spend more of their valuable time and resources doing what they do best—securing our federal information infrastructure.

---

[22] R. E. Chapman and Leng, *Cost-Effective Responses to Terrorist Risks in Constructed Facilities*, NISTIR 7073 (Gaithersburg, MD: National Institute of Standards and Technology, 2004).

References

ASTM International. *ASTM Standards on Building Economics,* 5th Edition. West Conshohocken, PA, 2002.

Chapman, Robert E., and Leng, C. J., Cost-Effective Responses to Terrorist Risks in Constructed Facilities, NISTIR 7073 (Gaithersburg, MD: National Institute of Standards and Technology, March 2004).

Federal Information Processing Standard 199, *Standards for Security Categorization of Federal Information and Information Systems,* February 2004.

Fuller, S. K. *Risk Exposure and Risk Attitude of Homeowners in Fire Protection Investment Decisions,* NISTIR 89-4212. Gaithersburg, MD: National Institute of Standards and Technology, 1989.

Government Accountability Office, *Information Technology Investment Management, A Framework for Assessing and Improving Process Maturity*, GAO-04-394-G, Version 1.1, March 2004.

Gass, S. I. *Decision Making, Models and Algorithms.* New York, NY: John Wiley and Sons, 1985.

Harker T. and Vargas, L. "The Theory of Ratio Scale Estimation: Saaty's Analytic Hierarchy Process." *Management Science,* Vol. 33, No. 11, 1987.

Hihn, J. M. and Johnson, C.R. "Evaluation Techniques for Paired Ratio-Comparison Matrices in a Hierarchical Decision Model," In *Measurement in Economics,* pp. 269-288. Edited by W. Eichhorn. Heidelberg, Germany: Physics Verlag, 1983.

Miller, G. A. "The Magical Number Seven, Plus or Minus Two: Some Limits on our Capacity for Processing Information." *Psychological Review,* Vol. 63, No. 2, 1956.

National Institute of Standards and Technology, *Integrating Security into the Capital Planning and Investment Control Process,* NIST Special Publication 800-65, January 2005

National Institute of Standards and Technology, *Recommended Security Controls for Federal Information Systems,* NIST Special Publication 800-53, February 2005.

Pulley, J., "Disciplinary Review: Top-notch Investment Review Boards Enforce IT Spending Discipline, but They're Hard to Find," *Federal Computer Week*, May 22, 2006. Available online at http://fcw.com/article94569-05-22-06-Print.

Saaty, T. L. *The Analytic Hierarchy Proces.* New York, NY: McGraw-Hill, 1980.

Saaty, T. L. *Decision Making for Leaders.* Gelmont, CA: Lifetime Learning Publications, 1982.

U.S. Office of Management and Budget, *Federal Participation in the Development and Use of Voluntary Consensus Standards and in Conformity Assessment Activities,* OMB Circular A-119, Washington, D.C., February 1998.

U.S. Department of Veterans Affairs, *VA Capital Investment Methodology Guide: FY 2005* (Draft), Washington, D.C., available at
http://www.va.gov/oaem/FY2005_Guide/FY2005_Capital_Investment_Guide.asp .

Appendix A Theoretical Foundation of the AHP

A.1 Estimation of Relative Weights of Decision Elements

The hierarchical structure of the Analytic Hierarch Process (AHP) arranges the elements of a complex selection problem into hierarchies and sub-hierarchies and compares the elements of each hierarchy in a pairwise fashion. The solution technique of the AHP takes as inputs the values generated by the pairwise comparisons and produces as outputs the relative weights of the hierarchy elements. The weights are calculated by the eigenvector method. To calculate the principal right eigenvector, the AHP needs a positive reciprocal matrix with n rows and n columns. The data from the pairwise comparisons produce such a matrix: the diagonal elements always equal one, and the lower-triangle elements are the reciprocals of those in the upper triangle. Table A.1 shows such a positive, reciprocal matrix for Level 1 of the hierarchy of Figure 3.1 in Chapter 3.

Table A.1 Judgment Matrix - Level 1

Risk-based Computer Security	Confidentiality	Integrity	Availability	A_i	P_i	p
Confidentiality	1	4	5	20.0	2.71	**0.68**
Integrity	1/4	1	2	0.50	0.79	0.20
Availability	1/5	1/2	1	0.10	0.46	0.12
				P = 3.97		1.00

To obtain the relative weights of the elements, the AHP normalizes the principal eigenvector and interprets it as the vector of priorities that indicates the importance of each criterion with respect to an element in the next higher level. An algorithm exists to estimate the principal eigenvector by iterative computation. For the IT security example, it is estimated as follows: For each row i of the matrix, take the product of the n entries in that row and denote it A_i. Then calculate the corresponding geometric mean P_i, where $P_i = \sqrt[n]{\prod_i}$. Normalize P_i by calculating $P = 3\ P_i$ and forming $p_i = P_i / P$. Each p_i is thus the ith priority or weight given to the ith element.

The last three columns in Table A.1 list the results of this approximation for the judgment matrix of Level 1 of the hierarchy example. The p_i column of the matrix shows that in this case confidentiality with a priority of 0.68, is the most important criterion, with respect to providing risk-based computer security. The decision-maker considers integrity, with a priority of 0.20, and availability, with a priority of 0.12, as less important in this example.

The above steps are repeated for all levels of the hierarchy for which pairwise comparisons have been made. Table A.2 shows the judgment matrices and the calculated priorities calculated from the pairwise comparisons for the investment alternatives in the lowest tier of the hierarchy of the IT security example described in Chapter 3. The priorities indicate which of the investment alternatives, A, B, or C, is preferred with respect to the criteria in Level 1.

Table A.2 Judgments and Estimated Priorities – Investment Alternatives

Confidentiality	A	B	C	A_i	P_i	p_i
A	1	5	4	20.0	2.71	**0.67**
B	1/5	1	1/3	0.07	0.41	0.10
C	1/4	3	1	0.75	0.91	0.23
				P =	4.03	1.00
Integrity	A	B	C	A_i	P_i	p_i
A	1	1/5	1/3	0.07	0.41	0.10
B	5	1	3	15.0	2.46	**0.64**
C	3	1/3	1	1.0	1.0	0.26
				P =	3.87	1.00
Availability	A	B	C	A_i	P_i	p_i
A	1	2	1/3	0.67	0.87	0.23
B	1/2	1	1/5	0.10	0.46	0.12
C	3	5	1	15.0	2.46	**0.65**
				P =	3.97	1.00

The priorities calculated from the pairwise comparison judgments in Table A.2 show that Investment A is preferred over the other two with respect to confidentiality (0.67), Investment B with respect to integrity (0.64), and Investment C with respect to availability (0.65). To help decide which investment to select, however, an overall rating of the three alternatives is necessary, that is, the results from all three tiers have to be aggregated.

A.2 Aggregation of Relative Weights and Ratings

All importance weights and preference ratings—whether developed through pairwise comparison or by directly using quantitative data—are "synthesized" by factoring the influence of the preceding levels into the decision. The result is an overall ranking of the investment alternatives in the lowest tier of the hierarchy.

To determine a ranking for each investment alternative, its Table A.2 priorities, p_i, are multiplied by the corresponding Level 1 priorities from Table A.1 and the products summed. Table A.3 shows the priorities for Level 1 and for the investment alternatives as well as the overall priority ranking.

Table A.3 Overall Priority Rankings for Investment Alternatives

Priorities	Confidentiality	Integrity	Availability	Overall Priority Ranking
Level 1	0.68	0.20	0.12	
Investment Alternatives A	0.67	0.10	0.23	0.51
Investment Alternatives B	0.10	0.64	0.12	0.21
Investment Alternatives C	0.23	0.26	0.65	0.28

The overall ranking of Investment A is calculated as a cross product as follows: 0.68(0.67) + 0.20(0.10) + 0.12(0.23) = 0.51; the overall rankings for Investments B and C, calculated in a like manner, are 0.21 and 0.28 respectively.[23] Investment A ranks highest, Investment C ranks second, and Investment B has the lowest overall priority ranking with respect to Cost-effective, Risk-Based Computer Security.

A.3 Theoretical Basis of the Pairwise Comparison Method

A.3.1 Relationship between Eigenvalues and Priorities

There are many methods for assigning weights to judgments and calculating the associated priorities for different alternatives. Some involve a simple weighting of criteria, such as the pairwise comparisons of the AHP, others involve more complex weighting methods such as predictability, correlation, or variance. Using graph theory, Saaty (1980) has shown that with a reciprocal, positive matrix, the eigenvector method produces estimates of priorities that correctly indicate the relative importance of each alternative with respect to the others.[24] The judgment matrix of the AHP is such a matrix. The theoretical foundation of the eigenvector method is explained in detail in Saaty (1982) and Harker and Vargas (1987)[25]. In general, if A is an $n \times n$ matrix, then a $n \times 1$ non-zero vector b is called an eigenvector of A if Ab is a scalar multiple of b, that is, $Ab = \lambda b$. The scalar λ is called an eigenvalue of A, and b is an eigenvector corresponding to λ. For practical applications usually only the eigenvector associated with the largest eigenvalue is needed. The AHP, for instance, calculates priorities by normalizing the elements of the eigenvector associated with the largest eigenvalue of the judgment matrix.

---

[23] If there are more than three tiers in the hierarchy, the ranking calculation is simply expanded to include in the cross products all corresponding, higher-tier priorities. In that case, the preferred alternative will be different.

[24] S. I. Gass, *Decision Making, Models and Algorithms* (New York, NY: John Wiley and Sons, 1985).

[25] Harker and Vargas, 1987.

A.3.2 Consistency

The relationship between the pairwise comparison values and the priorities is mathematically exact if the judgment matrix is a consistent matrix. For example, if the decision-maker says that Investment A is twice as likely to guarantee information integrity as Investment B and Investment B is three times as likely to guarantee information integrity as Investment C, he or she will also have to say that Investment A is six times more likely to guarantee information integrity as Investment C to be truly consistent. In situations where many elements have to be compared and where some of the judgments have to be subjective, it is more realistic to allow for some inconsistency. It has been shown that small deviations from consistent judgments do not change the priorities by much; information coming from all pairwise comparison values contributes to the calculation of the priorities.[26] In the case of a reciprocal matrix, small changes in some values will be offset by changes in other values because there are redundant judgments. Large inconsistencies, however, may reverse the ranking of decision alternatives. The AHP therefore includes a measure of the departure from consistency, called the consistency ratio (CR). The CR is calculated for each matrix at each level and then aggregated to provide a consistency measure for the entire hierarchy.

The consistency ratio is based on the magnitude of the largest eigenvalue of the matrix. The largest eigenvalue of a consistent, reciprocal matrix is equal to n, the number of rows and columns in the matrix; the eigenvalue of an inconsistent matrix is larger than n. The deviation from consistency can be represented by the Consistency Index (CI)

$$CI = |(\lambda_{max}-n)|/(n-1),$$

that is, the CI is the absolute value of the difference between the largest eigenvalue of an inconsistent matrix and the largest eigenvalue of a consistent matrix, divided by the number of degrees of freedom (n-1). The CI of the matrix is then compared with the Random Index (RI), an index calculated from a randomly generated reciprocal matrix of the same size and scale. The CR, the measure of inconsistency, is arrived at as follows:

$$CR = CI/RI.$$

A consistency ratio of 0.10 or less indicates a high level of consistency. While a consistency ratio of between 0.10 and 0.15 is considered acceptable, it indicates that a review of pairwise comparison judgments may be warranted. If it is higher than 0.15, it is advisable to reexamine the judgments and eliminate the most obvious inconsistencies.

λ_{max} can be approximated by multiplying the column sums of a judgment matrix by the corresponding priorities and adding the products, as follows:

$$\lambda_{max} = p_1 \Sigma a_{j1} + p_2 \Sigma a_{j2} + p_3 \Sigma a_{j3} + \ldots + p_n \Sigma a_{jn},$$

---

[26] Saaty, 1982, ch. 7

where *a* refers to the pairwise comparison judgments.

To illustrate how the consistency ratio is calculated, the Level 1 judgment matrix of the information security example (in Table A.1) will be used. The relevant values are shown in Table A.4.

Table A.4 Consistency Ratio for a Judgment Matrix

Risk-Based Computer Security	Confidentiality	Integrity	Availability	Priorities (p_i)
Confidentiality	1	4	5	0.68
Integrity	1/4	1	2	0.20
Availability	1/5	1/2	1	0.12
Column Sums	1.45	5.5	9.36	CR = 0.02

The CR is calculated as follows:

$$\lambda_{max} = 0.68(1.45) + 0.20(5.5) + 0.12(9.36) = 3.03^{[27]}$$
$$\text{Consistency Index} = |(3.03 - 3)|/(3-1) = 0.0131$$

For a matrix of size n = 3, the RI is 0.58.[28] Dividing the CI by the RI determines how consistent the judgments are:

$$\text{Consistency Ratio} = 0.0131/0.58 = 0.0226$$

The consistency ratio is less than 0.10 and therefore within the acceptable range. If the CR does not lie within the acceptable range of 0.10 – 0.15, performing a sensitivity analysis with revised values for some of the more ambiguous judgments might provide additional information and improve the consistency ratio.

---

[27] λ_{max} result, 3.03, calculated using unrounded values.
[28] Saaty, 1988, p. 21.

Appendix B Acronyms

AHP – Analytic Hierarchy Process

ASTM – American Society for Testing and Materials

C&A – Certification and Accreditation

CI – Consistency Index

CIO –Chief Information Officer

CR – Consistency Ratio

FIPS – Federal Information Processing Standard

GAO – Government Accountability Office

IRB – Investment Review Board

IT – Information Technology

ITIM – Information Technology Investment Management

NIST – National Institute of Standards and Technology

OMB – Office of Management and Budget

POA&M – Plan of Action and Milestones

RI – Random Index

www.ingramcontent.com/pod-product-compliance
Lightning Source LLC
Chambersburg PA
CBHW080604060326
40689CB00021B/4933